CALIFORNIA
NATIVE AMERICAN TRIBES

YUROK TRIBE

by
Mary Null Boulé

Illustrated by
Daniel Liddell

Merryant Publishing
Vashon, Washington

Book Number Twenty-six in a series of twenty-six

This series is dedicated to Virginia Harding, whose editing expertise and friendship brought this project to fruition.

Library of Congress Catalog Card Number: 92-61897

ISBN: 1-877599-48-4

Copyright © 1992, Merryant Publishing

7615 S.W. 257th St., Vashon, WA 98070.

FOREWORD

Native American people of the United States are often living their lives away from major cities and away from what we call the mainstream of life. It is, then, interesting to learn of the important part these remote tribal members play in our everyday lives.

More than 60% of our foods come from the ancient Native American's diet. Farming methods of today also can be traced back to how tribal women grew crops of corn and grain. Many of our present day ideas of democracy have been taken from tribal governments. Even some 1,500 Native American words are found in our English language today.

Fur traders bought furs from tribal hunters for small amounts of money, sold them to Europeans and Asians for a great deal of money, and became rich. Using their money to buy land and to build office buildings, some traders started business corporations which are now the base of our country's economy.

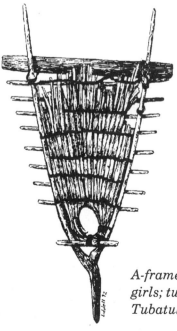

There has never been enough credit given to these early Americans who took such good care of our country when it was still in their care. The time has come to realize tribal contributions to our society today and to give Native Americans not only the credit, but the respect due them.

Mary Boulé

A-frame cradle for girls; tule matting. Tubatulabal tribe.

3

GENERAL INFORMATION

Out of Asia, many thousands of years ago, came Wanderers. Some historians think they were the first people to set foot on our western hemisphere. These Wanderers had walked, step by step, onto our part of the earth while hunting and gathering food. They probably never even knew they had moved from one continent to another as they made their way across a land bridge, a narrow strip of land between Siberia and what is now Russia, and the state of Alaska.

Historians do not know exactly how long ago the Wanderers might have crossed the land bridge. Some of them say 35,000 years ago. What historians do know is that these people slowly moved down onto land that we now call the United States of America. Today it would be very hard to follow their footsteps, for the land bridge has been covered with sea water since the thawing of the ice age.

Those Wanderers who made their way to California were very lucky, indeed. California was a land with good weather most of the year and was filled with plenty of plant and animal foods for them to eat.

The Wanderers who became California's Native Americans did not organize into large tribes like the rest of the North American tribes. Instead, they divided into groups, or tribelets, sometimes having as many as 250 people. A tribelet could number as few as three, to as many as thirty villages located close to each other. Some tribelets had only one chief, a leader who lived in the largest village. Many tribes had a chief for each village. Some leaders had no real power but were thought to be wise. Tribal members always listened with respect to what their chief had to say.

From 20 to 100 people could be living in one village, which usually had several houses. In most cases, these groups of people were related to each other. From five to ten people of one family lived in one house. For instance, a mother, a father, two or three children, a grandmother, or aunt or daughter-in-law might live together.

Village members together would own the land important to them for their well-being. Their land might include oak trees with precious acorns, streams and rivers, and plants which were good to eat. Streams and rivers were especially important to a tribe's quality of life. Water drew animals to it; that meant more food for the tribe to eat. Fish were a good source of food, and traveling by boat was often easier than walking long distances. Water was needed in every part of tribal life.

Village and tribelet land was carefully guarded. Each group knew exactly where the boundaries of its land were found. Boundaries were known by landmarks such as mountains or rivers, or they might also be marked by poles planted in the ground. Some boundary lines were marked by rocks, or by objects placed there by tribal members. The size of a territory had to be large enough to supply food to every person living there.

The California tribes spoke many languages. Sometimes villages close together even had a problem understanding one another. This meant that each group had to be sure of the boundaries of other tribes around them when gathering food. It would not be wise to go against the boundaries and the customs of neighbors. The Native Americans found if they respected the boundaries of their neighbors, not so many wars had to be fought. California tribes, in spite of all their differences, were not as warlike as other tribes in our country.

Not only did the California tribes speak different languages, but their members also differed in size. Some tribes were very tall, almost six feet tall. The shortest people came from the Yuki tribe which had territory in what is now Mendocino County. They measured only about 5'2" tall. All Native Americans, regardless of size, had strong, straight black hair and dark brown eyes.

TRADE

Trading between tribes was an important part of life. Inland tribes had large animal hides that coastal tribes wanted. By trading the hides to coastal groups, inland tribes would receive fish and shells, which they in turn wanted. Coastal tribes also wanted minerals and rocks mined in the mountains by inland tribes. Obsidian rock from the northern mountains was especially wanted for arrowheads. There were, as well, several minerals, mined in the inland mountains, which could be made into the colorful body paints needed for religious ceremonies.

Southern tribes particularly wanted steatite from the Gabrielino tribe. Steatite, or soapstone, was a special metal which allowed heat to spread evenly through it. This made it a good choice to be used for cooking pots and flat frying pans. It could be carved into bowls because of its softness and could be decorated by carving designs into it. Steatite came from Catalina Island in the Coastal Gabrielino territory. Gabrielinos found steatite to be a fine trading item to offer for the acorns, deerskins, or obsidian stone they needed.

When people had no items to trade but needed something, they used small strings of shells for money. The small dentalium shells, which came from the far distant Northwest coast, had great value. Strings of dentalia usually served as money in the Northern California tribes, although some dentalia was used in the Central California tribes.

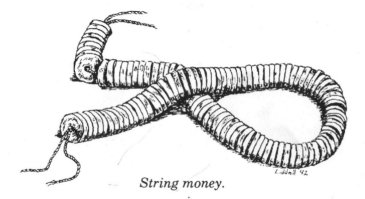

String money.

In southern California clam shells were broken and holes were bored through the center of each piece. Then the pieces were rounded and polished with sandstone and strung into strings for money. These were not thought to be as valuable as dentalia.

Strings of shell money were measured by tattoo marks on the trader's lower arm or hand.

Here is a sample of shell value:

A house, three strings
A fishing place, one to three strings
Land with acorn-bearing oak trees, one to five strings

A great deal of rock and stone was traded among the tribes for making tools. Arrows had to have sharp-edged stone for tips. The best stone for arrow tips was obsidian (volcanic glass) because, when hit properly, it broke off into flakes with very sharp edges. California tribes considered obsidian to be the most valuable rock for trading.

Some tribes had craftsmen who made knives with wooden handles and obsidian blades. Often the handles were decorated with carvings. Such knives were good for trading purposes. Stone mortars and pestles, used by the women for grinding grains into flour, were good trading items.

BASKETS & POTTERY

California tribal women made beautiful baskets. The Pomo and Chumash baskets, what few are left, show us that the women of those tribes might have been some of the finest basketmakers in the world. Baskets were used for gathering and storing food, for carrying babies, and even for hauling water. In emergencies, such as flooding waters, sometimes children, women, and tribal belongings crossed the swollen rivers and streams in huge, woven baskets! Baskets were so tightly woven that not a drop of water could leak from them.

Baskets also made fine cooking pots. Very hot rocks were taken from a fire and tossed around inside baskets with a looped tree branch until food in the basket was cooked.

Most baskets were made to do a certain job, but some baskets were designed for their beauty alone and were excellent for trading. Older women of a tribe would teach young girls how to weave baskets.

Pottery was not used by many California tribes. What little there was seems to have been made by those tribes living near to the Navaho and Mohave tribes of Arizona, and it shows their style. For example, pottery of the California tribes did not have much decoration and was usually a dull red color. Designs were few and always in yellow.

Ohlone hunter wearing deerskin camouflage.

Long thin coils of clay were laid one on top the other. Then the coils were smoothed between a wooden paddle and a small stone to shape the bowl. Pottery from California Native Americans has been described as light weight and brittle (easily broken), probably because of the kind of clay soil found in California.

HUNTING & FISHING

Tribal men spent much of their time making hunting and fishing tools. Bows and arrows were built with great care, to make them shoot as accurately as possible. Carelessly made hunting weapons caused fewer animals to be killed and people then had less food to eat.

Bows made by men of Southern California tribes were made long and narrow. In the northern part of the state bows were a little shorter, thinner, and wider than those of their northern neighbors. Size and thickness of bows depended on the size trees growing in a tribe's territory. The strongest bows were wrapped with sinew, the name given to animal tendons. Sinew is strong and elastic like a rubber band.

Arrows were made in many sizes and shapes, depending on their use. For hunting larger animals, a two-piece arrow was used. The front piece of the arrow shaft was made so that it would remain in the animal, even if the back part was removed or broken off. The arrowhead, or point, was wrapped to the front piece of the shaft. This kind of arrow was also used in wars.

Young boys used a simple wooden arrow with the end sharpened to a point. With this they could hunt small animals like birds and rabbits. The older men of the tribe taught boys how to make their own arrows, how to aim properly, and how to repair broken weapons.

Tribal men spent many hours making and mending fishing nets. The string used in making nets often came from the fibers of plants. These fibers were twisted to make them strong and tough, then knotted into netting. Fences, or weirs, that had one small opening for fish, were built across streams. As the fish swam through the opening they would be caught in netting or harpooned by a waiting fisherman.

Hooks, if used at all, were cut from shells. Mostly hooks could be found when the men fished in large lakes or when catching trout in high mountain areas. Hooks were attached to heavy plant fiber string.

Dip nets, made of netting attached to branches that were bent into a circle, were used to catch fish swimming near shore. Dip nets had long handles so the fishermen could reach deep into the water.

Sometimes a mild poison was placed on the surface of shallow water. This confused the fish and caused them to float to the surface of the water, where they could be scooped up by a waiting fisherman. Not enough poison was used to make humans ill.

Not all fishing was done from the shore. California tribes used two kinds of boats when fishing. Canoes, dug out of one half a log, were useful for river fishing. These were square at each end, round on the bottom, and very heavy. Some of them were well-finished, often even having a carved seat in them.

Today we think of "balsa" as a very lightweight wood, but in Spanish, the word balsa means "raft". That is why Spanish explorers called the Native American canoes, made from tule reeds, "balsa" boats.

Balsa boats were made of bundled tule reeds and were used throughout most of California. They made into safe, lightweight boats for lake and river use. Usually the balsa canoe had a long, tightly tied bundle of tule for the boat bottom and one bundle for each side of the canoe. The front of the canoe was higher than the back. Balsa boats could be steered with a pole or with a paddle, like a raft.

Men did most of the fishing, women were in charge of gathering grasses, seeds, and acorns for food. After the food was collected, it was either eaten right away or made ready for winter storage.

Except for a few southern groups, California tribes had permanent villages where they lived most of the year. They also had food-gathering places they returned to each year to collect acorns, salt, fish, and other foods not found near their villages.

FOOD

Many different kinds of plant food grew wild in California in the days before white people arrived. Berries and other plant foods grew in the mountains. Forests offered the local tribes everything from pine nuts to animals.

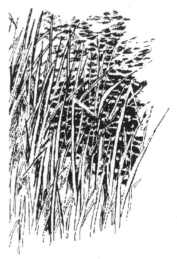

Native Americans found streams full of fish for much of the year. Inland fresh water lakes had large tule reeds growing along their shores. Tule could be eaten as food when plants were young and tender. More important, however, tule was used in making fabric for clothes and for building boats and houses. Tule was probably the most useful plant the California Native Americans found growing wild in their land.

Like all deserts, the one in southern California had little water or fish, but small animals and cactus plants made good food for the local tribes. They moved from place to place harvesting whatever was ripe. Tribal members always knew when and where to find the best food in their territory.

Acorns were the main source of food for all California tribes. Acorn flour was as important to the California Native Americans as wheat is to us today. Five types of California oak trees produced acorns that could be eaten. Those from black oak and tanbark oak seem to have been the favorite kinds.

Since some acorns tasted better than others, the tastiest ones were collected first. If harvest of the favorite acorn was poor some years, then less tasty acorns had to be eaten all winter long.

So important were acorns to California Indians that most tribes built their entire year around them. Acorn harvest marked the beginning of their calendar year. Winter was counted as so many months after acorn harvest, and summer was counted by the number of months before the next acorn harvest.

Acorn harvest ceremonies usually were the biggest events of the year. Most celebrations took place in mid-October and included dancing, feasts, games of chance, and reunions with relatives. Harvest festivals lasted for many days. They were a time of joy for everyone.

The annual acorn gathering lasted two to three weeks. Young boys climbed the oak trees to shake branches; some men used long poles to knock acorns to the ground. Women loaded the nuts into large cone-shaped burden baskets and carried them to a central place where they were put in the sun to dry.

Once the acorns were dried, the women carried them back to the tribe's permanent villages. There they lined special basket-like storage granaries with strong herbs to keep insects away, then stored the acorns inside. Granaries were placed on stilts to keep animals from getting into them and were kept beside tribal houses.

Preparing acorns for each meal was also the women's job. Shells were peeled by hitting the acorns with a stone hammer on an anvil (flat) stone. Meat from the nut was then laid on a stone mortar. A mortar was usually a large stone with a slight dip on its surface. Sometimes the mortar had a bottomless basket, called a hopper, glued to its top. This kept the acorn meat from sliding off the mortar as it was beaten.

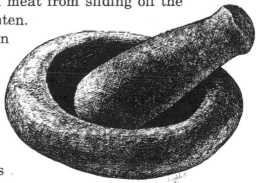

The meat was then pounded with a long stone pestle. Acorn flour was scraped away from the hopper's sides with a soaproot fiber brush during this process.

From there the flour was put into an open-worked basket and sifted. A fine flour came through the bottom of the basket, while the larger pieces were put back in the mortar for more pounding.

The most important process came after the acorn flour was sifted. Acorn flour has a very bitter-tasting tannin in it. This bitter taste was removed by a method called leaching. Many tribes leached the flour by first scooping out a hollow in sand near water. The hollow was lined with leaves to keep the flour from washing away. A great deal of hot water was poured through the flour to wash out (leach) the bitterness. Sometimes the flour was put into a basket for the leaching process, instead of using sand and leaves.

Finally the acorn flour was ready to be cooked. To make mush, heated stones were placed in the basket with the flour. A looped tree branch or two long sticks were used to toss the hot rocks around so the basket would not burn. When the mush had boiled, it could be eaten. If the flour and water mixture was baked in an earthen oven, it became a kind of bread. Early explorers wrote that it was very tasty.

Historians have estimated that one family would eat from 1500 to 2000 pounds of acorn flour a year. One reason California native Americans did not have to plant seeds and raise crops was because there were so many acorns for them to harvest each year.

Whether they ate fish or shellfish or plant food or animal meat, nature supplied more than enough food for the Native Americans who lived in California long ago. Many believed their good fortune in having fine weather and plenty to eat came from being good to their gods.

RELIGION

Tribal members had strong beliefs in the power of spirits or gods around them. Each tribe was different, but all felt the importance of never making a spirit angry with them. For that reason a celebration to thank the spirit-gods for treating them well, took place before each food gathering and before each hunting trip, and after each food harvest.

Usually spiritual powers were thought to belong to birds or animals. Most California tribespeople felt bears were very wicked and should not be eaten. But Coyote seems to have been a kind leader who helped them if they were in trouble, even though he seems to have been a bit naughty at times. Eagle was thought to be very powerful and good to native Americans. In some tribes, Eagle was almost as powerful as Sun.

Tribes placed importance on different gods, according to the tribe's needs. Rain gods were the most important spirits to desert tribes. Weather gods, who might bring less rain or warmer temperatures, were important to northern tribes. A great many groups felt there were gods for each of the winds: North, South, East and West. The four directions were usually included in their ceremonial dances and were used as part of the decorations on baskets, pots, and even tools.

Animals were not only worshipped and believed to be spirit-gods, like Deer or Antelope, but tribal members felt there was a personal animal guardian for each one of them. If a tribal member had a deer as guardian, then that person could never kill a deer or eat deer meat.

California Native Americans believed in life after death. This made them very respectful of death and very fearful of angering a dead person. Once someone died, the name of the dead person could never again be said aloud. Since it was easy to accidentally say a name aloud, the name was usually given to a new baby. Then the dead person would not become angry.

Shamans were thought to be the keepers of religious beliefs and to have the ability to talk directly to spirit-gods. It was the job of a village shaman to cure sick people, and to speak to the gods about the needs of the people. Some tribes had several kinds of shamans in one village. One shaman did curing, one scared off evil spirits, while another took care of hunters.

Not all shamans were nice, so people greatly feared their power. However, if shamans had no luck curing sick people or did not bring good luck in hunting, the people could kill them. Most shamans were men, but in a few tribes, women were doctors.

Most California tribal myths have been lost to history because they were spoken and never written down. The legends were told and retold on winter nights around the home fires. Sadly, these were forgotten after the missionaries brought Christianity to California and moved tribal members into the missions.

A few stories still remain, however. It is thought by historians that northwest California tribes were the only ones not to have a myth on how they were created. They did not feel that the world was made and prepared for human beings. Instead, their few remaining stories usually tell of mountain peaks or rivers in their own territory.

The central California tribes had creation stories of a great flood where there was only water on earth. They tell of how man was made from a bit of mud that a turtle brought up from the bottom of the water.

Many southwest tribes believed there was a time of no sky or water. They told of two clouds appearing which finally became Sky and Earth.

Throughout California, however, all tribes had myths that told of Eagle as the leader, Coyote as chief assistant, and of less powerful spirits like Falcon or Hawk.

Costumes for religious ceremonies often imitated these animals they worshipped or feared. Much time was spent in making the dance costumes as beautiful as possible. Red woodpecker feathers were so brilliant a color they were used to decorate religious headdresses, necklaces, or belts. Deerskin clothing was fringed so shell beads could be attached to each thin strip of leather.

Eagle feathers were felt to be the most sacred of religious objects. Sometimes they were made into whole robes.

Religious feather charm.

Usually, though, the feathers were used just for decorations. All these costumes were valuable to the people of each tribe. The village chief was in charge of taking care of the costumes, and there was terrible punishment for stealing them. Clothing worn everyday was not fancy like costuming for rituals.

Willow bark skirt.

CLOTHING

Central and southern California's fine weather made regular clothes not really very important to the Native Americans. The children and men went naked most of the year, but most women wore a short apron-like skirt. These skirts were usually made in two pieces, front and back aprons, with fringes cut into the bottom edges. Often the skirt was made from the inner bark of trees, shredded and gathered on a cord. Sometimes the skirt was made from tule or grass.

In northern California and in rainy or windy weather elsewhere in the state, animal-skin blankets were worn by both men and women. They were used like a cape and wrapped around the body. Sometimes the cape was put over one shoulder and under the other arm, then tied in front. All kinds of skins were used; deer, otter, wildcat, but sea-otter fur was thought to be the best. If the skin was from a small animal, it was cut into strips and woven together into a fabric. At night the cape became a blanket to keep the person warm.

Because of the rainy weather in northern California, the women wore basket caps all the time. Women of the central and south tribes wore caps only when carrying heavy loads, where the forehead had to be used as support. Then a cap helped keep too much weight from being placed on the forehead.

Most California people went barefoot in their villages. For journeys into rough land, going to war, wood gathering, or in colder weather, the tribesmen in central and northwest California wore a one-piece soft shoe with no extra sole, which went high up on the leg.

Southern California tribespeople, however, wore sandals most of the time, wearing high, soled moccasins only when they traveled long distances or into the mountains. Leggings of skin were worn in snow, and moccasins were sometimes lined with grass for more comfort and warmth.

VILLAGE LIFE

Houses of the California tribes were made of materials found in their area. Usually they were round with domed roofs. Except for a few tribes, a house floor was dug into the earth a few feet. This was wise, for it made the home warmer in winter and cooler in summer. It also meant that less material was needed to make house walls.

Framework for the walls was made from bendable branches tied to support poles. Some frames of the houses were covered with earth and grass. Others were covered with large slabs of redwood or pine bark. Central California

Split-stick clapper, rhythm instrument. Hupa tribe.

villagers made large woven mats of tule reed to cover the tops and sides of houses. In the warmer southern area, brush and smaller pieces of bark were used for house walls.

Most California Native American villages had a building called a sweathouse, where the men could be found when they were not hunting, fishing or traveling. It was a very important place for the men, who used it rather like a clubhouse. They could sweat and then scrape themselves clean with curved ribs of deer. The sweathouse was smaller than a family house. Normally it had a center pole framework with a firepit on the ground next to the pole. When the fire was lit, some smoke was allowed to escape through a hole at the top of the roof; however, most was trapped inside the building. Smoke and heat were the main reasons for having a sweathouse. Both were believed to be a way to purify tribal members' bodies. Sweathouse walls were mainly hard-packed earth. The heat produced was not a steam heat but came from a wood-fed fire.

In the center of most villages was a large house that often had no walls, just a roof held up with poles. It was here that religious dances and rituals were held, or visitors were entertained.

Dances were enjoyed and were performed with great skill. Music, usually only rhythm instruments, accompanied the dances. For some reason California Native Americans did not use drums to create rhythms for their dances. Three different kinds of rattles were used by California tribes.

One type, split-clap sticks, created rhythm for dancing. These were usually a length of cane (a hollow stick) split in half lengthwise for about two-thirds of its length. The part still uncut was tightly wound with cord so it would not split all the way. The stick was held at the tied end in one hand and hit against the palm of the other hand to make its sound.

A pebble-filled moth cocoon made rhythm for shaman duties. These could range from calling on spirits to cure illnesses, to performing dances to bring rain. Probably the best sounds to beat rhythm for songs and dances came from bundles of deer hooves tied together on a stick. These rattles have a hollow, warm sound.

The only really "musical" instrument found in California was a flute made of reed that was played by blowing across the edge of one end. Melodies were not played on any of these instruments. Most North American Indians sang their songs rather than playing melodies on music instruments.

Special songs were sung for each event. There were songs for healing sick people, songs for success in hunting, war, or marriage. Women sang acorn-grinding songs and lullabies. Songs were sung in sorrow for the dead and during story-telling times. Group singing, with a leader, was the favorite kind of singing. Most songs were sung by all tribe members, but religious songs had to be sung by a special group. It was important that sacred songs not be changed through the years. If a mistake was made while singing sacred music, the singer could be punished, so only specially trained singers would sing ritual songs.

All songs were very short, some of them only 20 to 30 seconds long. They were made longer by repeating the melodies over and over, or by connecting several songs together. Songs usually told no story, just repeated words or phrases or syllables in patterns.

Song melodies used only one or two notes and harmony was never added. Perhaps that is why mission Indians, at those missions with musician priests, especially loved to sing harmony in the church choirs.

Songs and dances were good methods of passing rich tribal traditions on to the children. It was important to tribal adults that their children understand and love the tribe's heritage.

Children were truly wanted by parents in most tribes and new parents carefully watched their tiny babies day and night, to be sure they stayed warm and dry. Usually a newborn was strapped into a cradle and tied to the mother's back so she could continue to work, yet be near the baby at all times. In some tribes, older children took care of babies of cradle age during the day to give the mother time to do all her work, while grandmothers were often in charge of caring for toddlers.

Children were taught good behavior, traditions, and tribal rules from babyhood, although some tribes were stricter than others. Most of the time parents made their children obey. Young children could be lightly punished, but in many tribes those over six or seven years old were more severely punished if they did not follow the rules.

Just as children do today, Native American youngsters had childhood traditions they followed. For instance, one tribal tradition said that when a baby tooth came out, a child waited until dusk, faced the setting sun and threw the tooth to the west. There is no mention of a generous tooth fairy, however.

Tribal parents were worried that their offspring might not be strong and brave. Some tribes felt one way to make their children stronger was by forcing them to bathe in ice cold water, even in wintertime. Every once in a while, for example, Modoc children were awakened from sleep and taken to a cold lake or stream for a freezing bath.

But if freezing baths at night were hard on young Native Americans, their days were carefree and happy. Children were allowed to play all day, and some tribes felt children did not even have to come to dinner if they didn't want to. In those tribes, children could come to their houses to eat anytime of the day.

The games boys played are not too different from those played today. Swimming, hide and seek among the tule reeds, a form of tetherball with a mud ball tied to a pole, and willow-javelin throwing kept boys busy throughout the day.

Fathers made their sons small bows and arrows, so boys spent much time trying to improve their hunting skills. They practised shooting at frogs or chipmunks. The first animal any boy killed was not touched or eaten by him. Others would carry the kill home to be cooked and eaten by villagers. This tradition taught boys always to share food.

Another hunting tool for boys was a hollowed-out willow branch. This became like a modern day beanshooter, only the Native American boys shot juniper berries instead of beans. Slingshots made good hunting weapons, as well.

Girls and boys shared many games, but girls playing with each other had contests to see who could make a basket the fastest, or they played with dolls made of tule. Together, young boys and girls played a type of ring-around-the-rosie game, climbed mountains, or built mud houses.

As children grew older, the boys followed their fathers and the girls followed their mothers as the adults did their daily work. Children were not trained in the arts of hunting or basketmaking, however, until they became teenagers.

HISTORY

Spanish missionaries, led by Fray Junipero Serra, arrived in California in 1769 to build missions along the coast of California. By 1823, fifty years later, 21 missions had been founded. Almost all of them were very successful, and the Franciscan monks who ran them were proud of how many Native Americans became Christians.

However, all was not as the monks had planned it would be. Native American people had never been around the diseases European white men brought with them. As a result, they had no immunity to such illnesses as measles, small pox, or flu. Too many mission Indians died from white men's diseases.

Historians figure there were 300,000 Native Americans living in California before the missionaries came. The missions show records of 83,000 mission Indians during mission days. By the time the Mexicans took over the missions from the Spanish in 1834, only 20,000 remained alive.

The great California Gold Rush of 1849 was probably another big reason why many of the Native Americans died during that time. White men, staking their claim to tribal lands with gold upon it, thought nothing of killing any California tribesman who tried to keep and protect his territory. Fifty-thousand tribal members died from diseases, bullets, or starvation between the gold Rush Days and 1870. By 1910, only 17,000 California Indians remained.

Although the American government tried to set aside reservations (areas reserved for Native Americans), the land given to the Indians often was not good land. Worse yet, some of the land sacred to tribes, such as burial grounds, was taken over by white people and never given back.

Sadly, mission Indians, when they became Christians, forgot the proud heritage and beliefs they had followed for thousands of years. Many wonderful myths and songs they had passed from one generation to the next, on winter nights so long ago, have been lost forever.

Today some 100,000 people can claim California Native American ancestors, but few pure-blooded tribespeople remain. Our link with the Wanderers, who came from Asia so long ago, has been forever broken.

The bullroarer made a deep, loud sound when whirled above the player's head. Tipai tribe.

Villages were usually built beside a lake, stream, or river. Balsa canoes are on the shore. Tule reeds grow along the edge of the water and are drying on poles on the right side of the picture.

Women preparing food in baskets, sit on tule mats. Tule mats are being tied to the willow pole framework of a house being built by one of the men.

YUROK TRIBE

INTRODUCTION

The Yurok (Yur' rock) tribe lived in the northwest corner of what is today California. Some of its people lived in villages along 45 miles of the lower Klamath River. The tribe was one of three tribes — Karok, Tolowa, and Yurok — that lived next to each other and shared many of the same customs. Each tribe had its own language, but tribal members spoke all three languages and there was much visiting among them.

Yurok territory also ran along the Pacific Coast from Little River in the north, to Trinidad Bay in the south, in addition to the tribe's inland territory along the Klamath River. Today the land would be in the northern part of Humboldt County and continue north through much of what is Del Norte County.

Archeologists determined the age of ancient Yurok artifacts (old tools and other objects dug from the ground) by giving them a carbon test. Their tests showed that the Yuroks had lived in their territory for at least 600 years by the time European explorers discovered them.

Tribal groups never called themselves by any name but 'the people.' However, Native Americans described neighboring groups of tribal people by where they lived, rather than giving the different groups personal names. Thus, the name Yurok came from a Karok word, *yúruk*, meaning 'down river.'

The main Yurok villages were found right on the beach between the modern city of Trinidad, north to the mouth of the Klamath River. Boundary lines between Yuroks and the Tolowa tribe, which was just north of them on the coast, were carefully marked to keep peace between them.

Boundary lines between Yuroks and the Hupa tribe, southeast of them, were not as plainly marked. There was even an area running between both groups' boundaries that was used by both tribes. From time to time, trouble between these two tribes did arise.

This northwestern California area had more rain and was cooler, even along the inland Klamath River banks, than most other California tribal areas. Because of the dampness, Yurok villages had sturdy houses which looked more like those of Northwest and Alaskan tribes.

VILLAGES

There was a total of 50 Yurok villages before white people arrived, including both the seacoast and the Klamath River areas. Small settlements of related tribal members clustered together to make a village. It was thought that by clustering the groups, tribelets could better protect themselves in case of invading warriors from other villages or tribes.

©92Liddell

Each village had some property that everyone owned. Acorn groves and food-gathering campsites, as well as whale rights, could be used by all villagers without them getting special permission. However, Yuroks had less village ownership than most other California tribes. The reason for this was their keen interest in owning their own personal property and becoming wealthy.

Village houses were wood, rectangular in shape, and built of split-cedar and redwood plank walls. Grass in the village area was often burned to keep the wooden village houses safe from wildfires, which sometimes threatened them.

Houses of wealthy inland villagers were built on the highest ground above the Klamath River. In rainy years, the river and its streams could flood as much as 70 feet above normal. Rich villagers, whose belongings were quite valuable, did not want to take a chance on losing their treasures to lowland floods every few years.

Poorer villagers lived along the banks of the river, since they had less to lose to a flood. Every Yurok village had a separate area for wealthy tribal members' homes.

Each village also had plank-roofed sweathouses used for ceremonies and dances, as well as for sweating. These village sweathouses were open to all village men, and to boys eight years and older.

Wealthy villagers had their own family sweathouses. Both men and women used these private sweathouses every day. One of the signs of a wealthy family was the attention paid to sweating, which they believed purified their bodies and minds.

VILLAGE LIFE

The village sweathouse was a busy place. Large wood fires were built, creating high enough temperatures inside for tribal members to sweat and cleanse themselves. Men also made and repaired their tools there. Others considered the sweathouse a place for sitting and talking between their fishing and hunting trips.

Each house was lived in and owned by a whole family. This could mean a married couple, their unmarried children, widow and widower relatives of the couple, and sometimes sons- and daughters-in-law.

A house was inherited by the children when, their parents died. A family might live in one dwelling house for many generations, because of tribal inheritance laws. The land upon which a home sat was far more valuable than the house itself.

Property (land and belongings) owned by tribal members was of the greatest importance to them. Villagers worked hard to gain wealth. For example, they placed exact value both on humans, like brides, as well as on treasured objects. Services, such as loaning money or objects to one another, or allowing the use of privately owned fishing and hunting areas, were also carefully 'priced.' Precise fines were set, too, for criminal acts such as one person causing injury to another.

Here are some samples of the value of Yurok possessions and punishment fines:

A house	3 money strings
A fishing place	1 to 3 money strings
Grove of acorns	1 to 5 money strings
A slave (a debtor)	1 or 2 money strings
Redwood canoe	12 money strings, or 10 large (or 60 small) woodpecker scalps
Killing an important man	15 money strings
Killing a regular villager	10 strings

Yuroks, and other tribal people throughout California, used

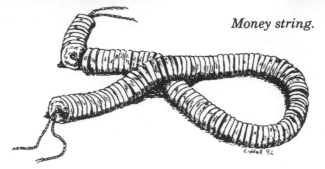

Money string.

stringed shells as we use coins and paper money today. Dentalium shells came from the shores of Vancouver Island, north of present-day Washington State. Dentalia came to California by being traded from tribe to tribe. These shells were the most valuable of all shells to Yuroks.

Shells were strung on vegetable fiber strings, all of them exactly the same length. Yurok men had marks tattooed on their upper arms just for measuring the length of dentalium strings.

When figuring the value of a string, tribal traders graded it by how well the shells on a string matched each other, on their color, as well as the string's length. Traders without products of equal value to trade for something they wanted, used shell money.

All village crimes were settled with shell money. If a poor criminal had no string money to pay his fine, he became a slave to his victim until the fine was paid in full. Slaves were not badly treated in this tribe, but more like poor relatives.

When a villager borrowed a tool from a rich person and lost or broke it, a fine had to be paid to the owner of the tool. If a borrower had no string money, he then had to work for the rich villager until the fine was paid.

Objects that were a sign of great wealth, other than string money, were 15-inch-long obsidian blades (especially a matched pair of them), albino (pure white) deerskins, and enough expensive dance costumes to put on a show with at least 11 costumed dancers.

Those villagers considered rich and important were religious performers, village leaders, shamans, and those who owned a great deal of land. Wealthy people made up about one third of the population of a village.

People from this group of villagers ate exotic foods from far-away places, had fine table manners, and bought food to host many ceremonial events. A person of wealth even had a speech accent different from that of other villagers.

VILLAGE LEADERS

Trained, wealthy villagers who did not become shamans were often busy in village government. They were sometimes on special councils where village quarrels and problems with other tribes were settled. Many important villagers were put on councils to organize ceremonies and dances.

There seems to have been no chief in charge of either the villages or the tribe. Groups of wealthy villagers appear to have taken care of all problems, even wars, within their councils.

FAMILY LIFE

Many marriages were arranged between two sets of parents while their children were still babies. The marriage ceremony took place when the children were grown. Most arranged marriages were arranged to combine the money of two families.

If a man decided not to marry the girl chosen for him when he was still a child, the bride price paid by his parents long ago was returned to the young woman's family. She was then free to marry someone of her choice.

A special older village woman was called upon to help a mother-to-be when a baby was due to be born. A newborn baby was carefully washed and wrapped in soft furs.

After the baby was wrapped, the older woman mixed hazelnut flour with warm water to make a milky drink. This drink was fed to the baby for a short time until the mother began to feed it herself. These older women, known as 'granny women,' stayed for several days to help care for each new baby.

As soon as possible, the child was placed in a basket shaped to keep the infant in a sitting position. A strap was fastened to the basket cradle so a new mother could either carry it on her back, set it up against a wall, or lay it flat when the baby slept. As a baby grew older, larger basket cradles were woven. Outgrown cradles were always burned.

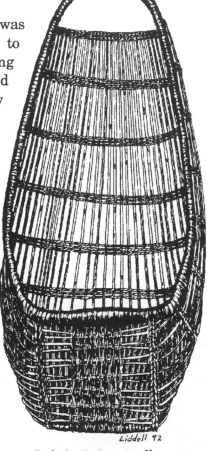

Among the richer villagers, when a child showed great promise he or she could become sponsored by an older, rich villager. Many times that sponsor was the child's mother or father. However, sometimes a sponsor was not a close relative.

Baby's sitting cradle.

SHAMANS

Rich-women curing doctors chose little girls, some as young as six years old, whom they trained for at least ten years. These chosen girls were taught the graces of good manners and helped the curing doctor as she performed her curing rituals.

Like the young girls, boys age six or over were sponsored by older rich men in the village. First a boy trainee was taught how to make bows and arrows and to chip obsidian arrow points. At about the age of eight, the young boy would begin going with his sponsor to the rich man's own sweathouse to start his training in tribal law.

This training continued for ten years, just like a girl's shaman training. At age 16, the boy tested his strength and intelligence by going alone into the high mountains for eight to twelve days.

If the young man received what he believed to be a supernatural 'vision' on this difficult journey, he might also train to become a shaman. Otherwise he would use his training for tribal leadership after he became an adult.

Both men and women shamans (curing doctors) had every chance to become some of the richest people in the village. Their job was to cure sick villagers, and for each cure a great deal of money or property was paid, especially to a successful shaman.

Women shamans did their healing in a different way from men. A woman shaman would announce what 'pain' was causing illness in a villager, then begin to sing and dance. At certain times the woman doctor would suck on areas of the body where she felt the 'pain' was located. This continued for many hours until the patient began to recover or the shaman coughed up what she called the 'pain' so the patient could begin to get well

Men shamans used many kinds of herbs, roots, and a few minerals in curing sick people. They, as well as the women, were paid before any curing ritual took place, and if the patient died in spite of the ritual, a shaman had to return all money paid to him in advance.

These tribal doctors owned their own medicine recipes, and when they died, one of their children, or another close relative, inherited the curing secrets.

Often, poor villagers did not have enough money to pay shamans when they were called to cure sick family members. In that case, they would pay a doctor with pieces of property they owned. If shamans were good at removing pain, they could become very rich.

Over the years, shamans would become owners of the best village property and other treasures. When shamans died, their children inherited all their parents' property. Because of tribal inheritance laws, later generations of shamans' families could become very wealthy, indeed.

DEATH RITUALS

The death of a villager was celebrated with rituals and ceremonies. If a villager died inside a house, the body was never carried out through a doorway. Either it was removed through a window or lifted out of the house through a hole made in the roof. Ashes were sprinkled around the opening after a body had been removed. As late as 1969, this custom was sometimes still being followed.

Bodies were buried on family property, and a fence decorated with feathers was put up around the grave. Clothing and other belongings of the dead person were placed on top of the grave.

The widows, or widowers, stayed beside their mates' graves for several nights following the burial. All remaining living relatives wore braided grass necklaces until they finally fell apart and dropped off, months later.

MYTHS AND BELIEFS

Yurok people thought of the earth as an island in the ocean. Sky was believed to be a domed cover over the earth. Waves in the ocean were said to be caused by the sky cover moving up and down all the time, causing the water to form waves.

This tribe had fearful respect for dogs, believing that dogs should not be spoken to directly. If someone did make the mistake of speaking to a dog, and the dog barked back, it was believed that person might die.

Because of this belief, tribal members never drank from the Klamath River. They feared someone may have thrown a dead dog into the river upstream, and the dog's supernatural power might have poisoned the water.

Myths were not so much stories as they were tales to explain how or why things were a certain way. One Yurok tale tells of Sea Otter woman who was to marry Kingfisher (a bird). However, Sea Otter woman's bride price was so large that Kingfisher had to search the earth to find enough money to buy her.

Seal and Sea Lion were in the sweathouse singing a song about Kingfisher's long trip and how they hoped he would die, when Kingfisher walked in and heard them.

Kingfisher was very angry, and in revenge set the sweathouse on fire. The arms of both Seal and Sea Lion were burned off short, and that is why today they have flippers instead of arms, and why Sea Lion is black on his shoulders.

GATHERING AND PREPARING FOOD

Women gathered all plant foods, the most important of which were acorns. Acorns were gathered in oak groves each autumn and carried back to winter villages in large burden baskets worn on women's backs. It took many trips to get enough nuts in village granaries to feed a family through the winter.

Burden basket.

Shelling and grinding acorns in stone mortars and pestles was an everyday job for women. After leaching the flour of the ground acorns (Chapter One, page 12), it was made into mush or bread.

During the growing season, wild berries were gathered and eaten fresh or sun-dried, pounded into flour, then moistened with water to make a dough that could be stored. Whenever a tasty drink was wanted, water was added to a piece broken from the stored chunk of dough.

Roots were dug from the ground with tall hardwood digging sticks which had sharp points on both ends. Bulbs and roots collected this way were prepared and cooked for eating much as we serve potatoes today. Seedbeater baskets were used to collect grass seeds, which were ground to a mealy flour and cooked into mush.

Food like mush was cooked in a boiling basket. This basket was so tightly woven by the women, that water and flour did not leak from it. Cooking was done by placing water and red hot rocks from the fire into a boiling basket with the food to be cooked. Women tossed the rocks with two sticks, or a looped branch, to keep the basket from being burned until the food was done.

More than half of what the Yuroks ate was fish, or other river and ocean life. Freshwater and saltwater mussels (shellfish), salmon, sturgeon, eel, and sea lions were eaten fresh-cooked or dried and stored for winter meals. Seaweed and kelp furnished salt for seasoning plant foods.

Salmon not eaten fresh was sun-dried and stored in baskets, each layer of fish separated by leafy bay tree twigs to keep out insects. As much as 2,000 pounds of salmon were caught and eaten by a family throughout the year.

FISHING AND HUNTING

Salmon was so important to the Yuroks that each year a first-salmon ceremony was celebrated as the first run began. Usually the ritual consisted of prayers being said over a specially-caught salmon. The fish was cooked and divided among the village men, each man eating only one bite of the ceremonial fish. No fish could be caught by tribal fishermen until this ceremony had been performed.

Tribal belief said if anyone did eat salmon before the ceremony, the spirit-gods would see to it that there would not be enough salmon for the tribe for a whole year. For this reason, punishment was very harsh to anyone who disobeyed this law.

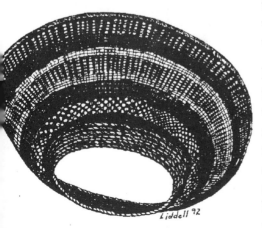

Dip nets were made by attaching netting to a branch which had been bent into a circle. A handle was tied to this kind of net so it could be used to catch fish swimming close to a river bank. Fishermen used harpoons to spear larger fish.

Yurok twined basket hopper.

They were speared from sturdy redwood dugout canoes made by this tribe.

In smaller streams, weirs (dams of stones, brush, and sticks) were built across the water. One opening was left for fish, and either a cone-shaped basket trap was fastened to the opening, or a fisherman stood over it ready to spear fish as they tried to swim through.

Traps, snares, and bows and arrows were used by village men when they hunted for larger animals. At least two types of wooden bows were made. The strongest bow had stretchy sinew (animal tendons) glued to the back of the bow to make it more bendable. The other kind of bow was made of wood wrapped in vegetable-fiber cord. Bows were strung with either deer sinew or cord.

Long, one-piece wooden arrow shafts, with fire-hardened sharp points at one end, were used for hunting animals. Shorter arrows, made of two pieces, were used in fighting wars and battles. The main shaft of this shorter arrow was made from hollow cane, and a pocket was put into one end. A thinner front shaft, with a stone point glued and tied to one end, fit into the pocket.

Only the arrow's front shaft remained in a target when it was hit; while the main shaft could be used over and over again.

No tribesman went on a hunt without following all the tribal customs. A most important ritual was sweating, believed to be needed to purify bodies for such an important mission as hunting for food. Ritual prayers and fasting (going without food for a period of time) also were thought to be helpful in making sure a hunt would be successful.

Some Yurok hunters were excellent marksmen. One visitor to a Yurok village, over one hundred years ago, wrote about a contest he had seen. From a distance of twenty feet, one tribal man hit a moving object about the size of a dime with

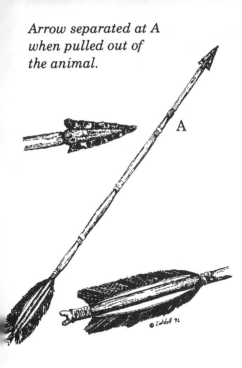

Arrow separated at A when pulled out of the animal.

his arrows, six times out of ten. Yurok men hunted more for the deer's skin than for its meat, since they liked fish as food better than they did deer.

CLOTHING

Men wore buckskin loin-cloths some of the time, but usually men and children went without clothes. In cooler weather, men and women wore capes or blankets of two deer hides sewn together.

Women always wore two-piece buckskin skirts with the back aprons larger than the front. The narrow front apron was plain buckskin for everyday wear. For dance events, the front panel was decorated with fringes, shell beads, juniper-berry beads, and abalone shells. Richer women wore valuable dentalium shell necklaces to dances.

Women wore their hair parted in the middle and tied into two soft ponytails, which hung in front of the shoulders. Each ponytail was tied with otter-skin strips. Women used deer-bone combs to comb their hair dry after washing it. This kept the hair straight and glossy.

Women wore basket caps on the tops of their heads. Not only did caps keep their heads dry in the Yuroks' rainy climate, but they protected women's foreheads whenever they carried heavy burden baskets on their backs. Attached to the baskets were netting or deerhide strips called tumplines. These tumplines were placed across women's foreheads to take some of the weight of their loads off their backs.

Moccasins of soft, tanned deerhide were worn, more by the women than the men. These were one-piece, with a single seam up the front of the moccasin and another seam up the back of the heel. A self-knotted deerskin thong wrapped a moccasin to the foot.

HISTORY

Most historians agree that white people did not visit the Yurok tribe until about 1775, when white traders exchanged iron, needed for tribal tools, for coast tribal hunters' animal skins. In 1827, the Hudson Bay fur traders visited Klamath River villages for the first time.

In 1850, many gold miners tore through Yurok territory looking for gold. The miners were greedy and took tribal land as their own, causing battles to be fought between miners and Yurok warriors.

The Yuroks, however, more than other California tribes, had several important white settlers on their side. These settlers helped tribal members keep some tribal land and saw to it that tribal men were given the right to vote in American elections some 20 years before other California Native Americans were allowed to vote.

In the late 1800s, the United States government gave a large piece of land along the upper Klamath River to Yurok people. Many Yuroks moved to this area and are still there today.

Before the 1850 Gold Rush, the population of full-blooded Yuroks was nearly 3,000. The tribe today still has about the same number of members living in, or near, their ancient territory. However, none are known to be full-blooded Yuroks.

Even so, some of the ancient Yurok customs continue to be followed. In the 1960s, there were a few boys who were being trained by older tribal members, just as in ancient days. A popular game called *shinney* , much like our present-day field hockey, was still being played in the 1970s. Today, tribal dancers still organize feasts and such dances as the Brush Dance, Jumping Dance, and Deerskin Dance.

It is good to learn that the Yuroks have been able to keep in touch with their heritage as much as they have. Certainly, it helps those who visit them to better understand ancient Yurok culture.

Woman with basket hat as described on page 39.

YUROK TRIBE

OUTLINE

I. Introduction
    A. Tribe location in California
        1. How long the tribe stayed in its territory
    B. Meaning of name
    C.Territory description
        1. Boundary lines
        2. Neighboring tribes
    E. Climate
II. Villages
    A. Number and location of villages
    B. Shared village property
    C. House descriptions
    D. Wealthy and poorer areas of village
    E. Sweathouse descriptions
III. Village life
    A. Sweathouse activity
    B. Family members living in houses
    C. Inheriting property
    D. Value of property
        1. Human
        2. Objects
        3. Dentalia bead money used in trading
    E. Punishing criminals
        1. Fines
IV. Village leaders
    A. Power and wealth of leaders
    B. Training for leadership
V. Family life
    A. Marriages and marriage customs
    B. Childbirth customs
        1. 'Granny women'
        2. Cradles
    C. Childhood and sponsors

GLOSSARY

AWL: a sharp, pointed tool used for making small holes in leather or wood

CEREMONY: a meeting of people to perform formal rituals for a special reason; like an awards ceremony to hand out trophies to those who earned honors

CHERT: rock which can be chipped off, or flaked, into pieces with sharp edges

COILED: a way of weaving baskets which looks like the basket is made of rope coils woven together

DIAMETER: the length of a straight line through the center of a circle

DOWN: soft, fluffy feathers

DROUGHT: a long period of time without water

DWELLING: a building where people live

FLETCHING: attaching feathers to the back end of an arrow to make the arrow travel in a straight line

GILL NET: a flat net hanging vertically in water to catch fish by their heads and gills

GRANARIES: basket-type storehouses for grains and nuts

HERITAGE: something passed down to people from their long-ago relatives

LEACHING: washing away a bitter taste by pouring water through foods like acorn meal

MORTAR: flat surface of wood or stone used for the grinding of grains or herbs with a pestle

PARCHING: to toast or shrivel with dry heat

PESTLE: a small stone club used to mash, pound, or grind in a mortar

PINOLE: flour made from ground corn

INDIAN RESERVATION: land set aside for Native Americans by the United States government

RITUAL: a ceremony that is always performed the same way

SEINE NET: a net which hangs vertically in the water, encircling and trapping fish when it is pulled together

SHAMAN: tribal religious men or women who use magic to cure illness and speak to spirit-gods

SINEW: stretchy animal tendons

STEATITE: a soft stone (soapstone) mined on Catalina Island by the Gabrielino tribe; used for cooking pots and bowls

TABOO: something a person is forbidden to do

TERRITORY: land owned by someone or by a group of people

TRADITION: the handing down of customs, rituals, and belief, by word of mouth or example, from generation to generation

TREE PITCH: a sticky substance found on evergreen tree bark

TWINING: a method of weaving baskets by twisting fibers, rather than coiling them around a support fiber

NATIVE AMERICAN WORDS WE KNOW AND USE

PLANTS AND TREES
hickory
pecan
yucca
mesquite
saguaro

ANIMALS
caribou
chipmunk
cougar
jaguar
opossum
moose

STATES
Dakota – friend
Ohio – good river
Minnesota – waters that
   reflect the sky
Oregon – beautiful water
Nebraska – flat water
Arizona
Texas

FOODS
avocado
hominy
maize (corn)
persimmon
tapioca
succotash

GEOGRAPHY
bayou – marshy body of
   water
savannah – grassy plain
pasadena – valley

WEATHER
blizzard
Chinook (warm, dry wind)

FURNITURE
hammock

HOUSE
wigwam
wickiup
tepee
igloo

INVENTIONS
toboggan

BOATS
canoe
kayak

OTHER WORDS
caucus – group meeting
mugwump – loner politician
squaw – woman
papoose – baby

CLOTHING
moccasin
parka
mukluk – slipper
poncho

BIBLIOGRAPHY

Cressman, L.S. *Prehistory of the Far West.* Salt Lake City, Utah: University of Utah Press, 1977.

Heizer, Robert F., volume editor. *Handbook of North American Indians, volume 8.* Washington, DC: Smithsonian Institution, 1978.

Heizer, Robert F. and Elsasser, Albert B. *The Natural World of the California Indians.* Berkeley and Los Angeles, CA; London, England: University of California Press, 1980.

Heizer, Robert F. and Whipple, M.A. *The California Indians.* Berkeley and Los Angeles, CA; London, England: University of California Press, 1971.

Heuser, Iva. *California Indians.* PO Box 352, Camino, CA 95709: Sierra Media Systems, 1977.

Macfarlen, Allan and Paulette. *Handbook of American Indian Games.* 31 E. 2nd Street, Mineola, N.Y. 11501: Dover Publications, 1985.

Murphey, Edith Van Allen. *Indian Uses of Native Plants.* 603 W. Perkins Street, Ukiah, CA 95482: Mendocino County Historical Society, copyright renewal, 1987.

National Geographic Society. *The World of the American Indians.* Washington, DC: National Geographic Society reprint, 1989

Thompson, Lucy, *The Training and Practices of Yurok Female Spiritual Doctors,* Shaman's Drum, Number 26, Winter, 1991-1992, p33.

Tunis, Edwin. *Indians.* 2231 West 110th Street, Cleveland, OH: The World Publishing Company, 1959.

Weatherford, Jack. *Native Roots.* 201 E. 50th Street, New York, N.Y.: Crown Publishers, Inc., 1991.

Credits:
Island Industries, Vashon Island, Washington 98070
Dona McAdam, Mac on the Hill, Seattle, Washington 98109

Acknowledgements:
Richard Buchen, Research Librarian, Braun Library,
Southwest Museum
Special thanks